Contents

Catching a cold

I'm Tessa. I've got a runny nose, and I've been whispering and giggling with my friend all through class.
Now I feel sick . . .

Illnesses like coughs, colds and flu are caused by germs. Germs spread by close contact - coughing, breathing, sneezing, all spread germs.

Passing it on!

I'm Abi, Tessa's friend.
I feel poorly, too.
Mum's kept me off
school today.

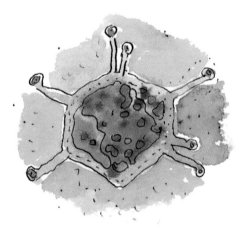

Germs are tiny living things, too
small to see just using our eyes.
A flu germ looks like this
through a microscope.

Germs like warm places to live
in – like people's bodies!

8

9

I'm Maggie, Abi's mum.
I've caught the bug now!
Flu always gives me
an upset tummy.
Thank goodness Abi's
dad is coming home . . .

Germs can affect people in different ways.

Always wash your hands after going to the loo. You'll wash off any germs as well as dirt.

11

Coughs and sneezes

I'm Mo, Abi's dad.
I'm glad I left work early -
I'm all stuffed up!
Aahhhahhchooo!

Germs can spread easily by coughing and sneezing. Put your hand to your mouth when you cough, or sneeze into a hanky to help stop germs spreading.

I'm Dave - the taxi driver. I can't manage my tea. I feel really dodgy! I'm always catching stuff off my customers.

Your body fights diseases best if you have a healthy diet, not just lots of junk food and sweets.

Eat plenty of fresh fruit and vegetables - the vitamins they contain, particularly vitamin C, can protect you against colds.

16

Stay in bed

I'm Mary, Dave's wife.
I feel terrible! I know I
shouldn't be up but we've
no milk or anything . . .

If you do get sick,
you need to rest.
This lets your body
concentrate on
making you better.

I'm Misha. I run the shop.
I feel hot and dizzy and I
can't stop coughing!

Sometimes, you have
a temperature when
your body is trying to
fight off germs.

18

19

At the doctor's

I'm Conner.
I feel like rubbish . . .
I don't know where I
caught this bug. Now
I've got to see the doctor.

You can pick up germs just about
anywhere, particularly indoors: in
shops, in buses, in the classroom
– even in doctors' waiting rooms.

21

It's me, Tessa, again. Mum's getting me some medicine. The doctor said it will help keep my temperature down. I hope it tastes nice!

Sometimes when we are sick, medicine will help us feel better.

Medicines and tablets are not sweets and can be dangerous. NEVER take them unless a grown-up gives them to you.

The best medicine

Abi here. The doctor says the best medicine for me is bed, lots to drink and lots of fresh fruit.

Although doctors do give you medicine when a cold turns nasty – they often prefer to let your body heal itself.

You need to drink lots of water when you've got a cold.

25

Germ ideas

Find out more about germs, feeling sick and, most importantly, staying healthy.

The history of a cold

If you or someone you know catches a cold, work out where it came from and who else caught it. Make a diagram to show the cold's history.

Watch it grow

Germs are everywhere - and they are not all bad! We use a type of germ to make cheese and yogurt.

Stir a teaspoon of natural yogurt into a cup of milk and leave in a warm place for a day or two. The germs in it will make more yogurt! Don't eat it, though. Some nasty germs may get in, too.

Design a poster

Eating fresh fruit and vegetables helps us to fight off colds. Make a poster telling everyone to eat more of them!

Be safe!

Remember, never take medicine or pills unless a grown-up says you can.

Germ words and index